The Path that Runs by the Church

Lois Rock

Illustrated by Louise Comfort

LION
Children's Books

Introduction

This book has been written to introduce school-age children to the pattern of the church year and the layout of a typical rural parish church.

The setting is a village community with its own little church and church school. The path from the houses to the school runs close to the church and so, through the changing seasons of the year, the children see some of the activity going on around the church as they pass by.

Sometimes the school is invited to the church; and at other times, people from the church go to the school.

In this way, the children learn even more about the building and the festivals of the Christian year.

The book also introduces three children who go to the church on Sundays, providing a glimpse through their eyes of what happens on those occasions.

I hope that all readers – teachers, parents and children – will also find it an endearing glimpse of the everyday life of a school!

Text by Lois Rock
Illustrations copyright © 2001 Louise Comfort
This edition copyright © 2001 Lion Publishing
Photography by John Williams Studios, Thame, except for cover: palm branches; introduction page: branches; contents page: palm branches; and photography on pages 16, 18, 19 (flowers) all by Mark Mason, Oxford

The moral rights of the author and illustrator have been asserted

Published by
Lion Publishing plc
Sandy Lane West, Oxford, England
www.lion-publishing.co.uk
ISBN 0 7459 4188 5

First edition 2001
10 9 8 7 6 5 4 3 2 1 0

A catalogue record for this book is available from the British Library

Typeset in 18/21 Baskerville MT Schoolbook
Printed and bound in Singapore

Contents

1 The Village of Clove

The village of Clove is very old.

The oldest building is the church: its thick stone walls were built a thousand years ago.

The oldest living thing is the yew tree by the church door. When the builders left the church a thousand years ago, it was just a seedling.

Generations of children have watched it grow.

The next oldest tree near the church is an oak. It was planted a hundred and fifty years ago, on the day Clove's little school opened for children.

Nowadays, most of the children in Clove live in the newest houses, which are only twenty years old.

To get to school each day, they walk along the path that goes by the oak, by the yew and by the church.

The school year starts in September, so that is when the children begin to find out about the church year.

2 Thinking About Harvest

The children walk to school. In people's gardens, runner beans hang from tall vines. Tomatoes and marrows and pumpkins ripen in the golden sunshine.

One garden has an apple tree. It overhangs the path. Tiny green windfalls lie on the path.

At the side door to the church, people are busy shaking out carpets and dusting brightly coloured cushions.

'We're getting ready for harvest festival,' they say.

'We hope you'll be bringing harvest gifts, like last year.'

'Of course,' answer the older children.

3 Harvest Gifts

One sunny afternoon, two weeks later, the children walk from school to the church.

They bring their harvest gifts of food and flowers.

Some of the gifts have been bought from a shop.

Some of the gifts have been made at home.

Some of the gifts have been grown in gardens.

'This is a very grand door,' says a boy called Daniel as he goes in.

Above him is an arch shaped like half a circle. It has fancy patterns on it.

The door is dark with iron hinges and an iron latch.

4 The Harvest-time Church

All the children tiptoe up a narrow walkway between rows of wooden seats. The carpet on the floor is one they saw being cleaned.

'You're walking up the aisle between the pews,' explains a lady.

They reach some steps. Here they lay their gifts.

Then they begin to chatter.

'I can hear my voice echo!' calls a girl. 'It's going up to the ceiling and back.'

'Hush,' says her friend. 'You have to be quiet and respectful in church.

'Why?' asks the girl.

'Because the building is old and valuable,' says one of the children.

'Because grown-ups say so,' adds another.

'Because it's a special place,' says a third. Her name is Sophie and she goes to church every Sunday with her mum and dad.

The church lady chuckles. 'I think it's a special place too,' she says. 'It's a place set aside for people to worship God. Sometimes they are quiet – and sometimes they're not!'

5 The Harvest Festival

The next day comes, and the school harvest festival begins after lunch.

The children sit in the front pews of the church. The parents and grandparents and carers and friends sit in the pews behind.

'The singing group is going to sit in the choir stalls,' announces the headteacher. The singing group takes its place in the seats above the steps where the gifts are laid.

A wooden screen decorated with flowers stands between the choir stalls and the rest of the church. The singers peek through.

A lady leads the service. She says she is the curate at the church, but everyone knows her as Sophie's mum.

Everyone takes part. Some classes chant a poem about harvest. Others read prayers.

The coloured cushions are there for people who want to kneel when they say a prayer. The cushions are pretty, but not very soft.

Year 3 have dressed up as vegetables and do a dance.

The singing group sings three songs. At the end, everyone stands up and sings a harvest hymn.

'We will have another harvest festival at our service here on Sunday,' says the lady curate. 'Then, on Monday, Year 6 will be helping take the gifts of food to people in Clove. I am so glad that we have food from the world's harvests to share.'

6 An October Funeral

The weeks go by, and the trees around Clove turn red and gold. Half-term is a windy week and many of the leaves are blown off the trees.

When the children return to school, they see pumpkins carved into faces outside several houses.

'For Halloween,' explains one of the mums. 'On Halloween, the pumpkins will be used as lanterns, with a candle inside.'

Later that week is Halloween. Some children go to school in fancy costumes. As they walk home, the sky is already quite dark and some of the pumpkin lanterns have been lit. 'They look spooky!' laughs a boy.

What they see in the churchyard as they go by makes them stop. There has been a funeral. People are huddled together around the vicar, watching as a coffin is lowered into the ground.

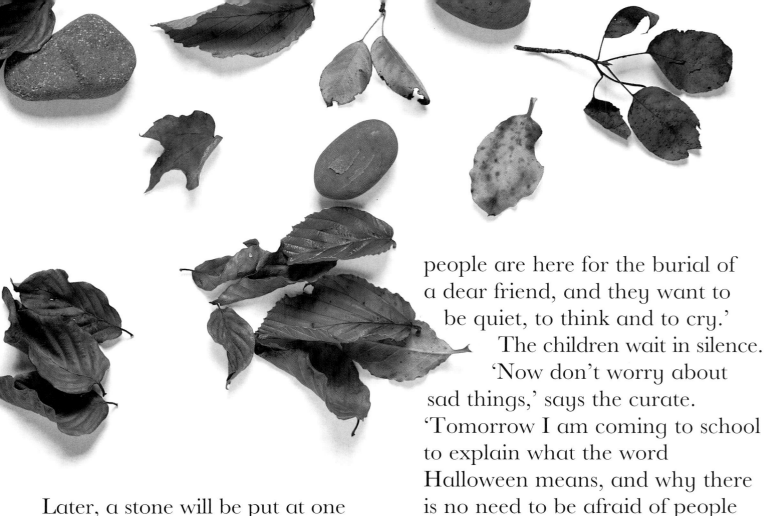

Later, a stone will be put at one end to mark the place.

'We saw the black car carrying the coffin,' whisper two girls. 'It went past our classroom window an hour ago.'

'I know who died. It's my Gran's best friend,' says a boy called Daniel. 'She was a nice lady. Now my Gran is going to look after her dog.'

Everyone goes very quiet. The lady curate comes to speak to the children. 'Can you wait a moment?' she asks. 'The people are here for the burial of a dear friend, and they want to be quiet, to think and to cry.'

The children wait in silence. 'Now don't worry about sad things,' says the curate. 'Tomorrow I am coming to school to explain what the word Halloween means, and why there is no need to be afraid of people dying, or of the spooky stories people tell about this night.'

7 All Saints and All Souls

When everyone meets in the hall the next morning, 1 November, the curate explains.

'Last night, I know some of you enjoyed some Halloween traditions – like "trick or treat". Those traditions are very, very old. They go back hundreds of years to when people had a coming-of-winter festival on 1 November called Samhain.

'Then people brought the news of Christianity. They replaced the old festival with a new one, called All Saints' Day. The night before was also given a new name – Halloween. "Hallow" is an old word for saint. "E'en" means "Eve", or "night before", as in Christmas Eve. So the word Halloween means "the night before All Saints' Day".

'A saint is someone who has lived a shining life, following the example of Jesus Christ. Some saints are remembered on special days…'

'Like Saint David on 1 March,' says a girl in Year 6.

'And Saint Francis who loved the birds and animals,' says a boy.

'Yes, his day is on 4 October,' says the curate. And all the saints are remembered today, on All Saints' Day.'

Daniel lifts his hand. 'My gran said that the lady who was buried yesterday was a saint, because she was always so kind and nothing was too much trouble if people needed help.'

'Quite right,' says the curate. 'The special book we read in church, the Bible, says that everyone who follows Christ is a saint. But only a few are officially named as saints. Anyway, the next day is called All Souls' Day, when we remember the people who have died. Christians believe that after death, their friends are safe with God for ever.'

It is a happy thought. The churchyard seems a brighter place that afternoon.

The next day, on All Souls' Day, the children see that many of the graves have fresh flowers on them, for many people have come to remember with love and affection the names of people who have lived and died in their village of Clove.

Now it is near the end of November.

One day, as the children are on their way to school, they see two people with huge bags full of greenery. They are going to the church.

That morning, everyone is told to keep their coats on and go to the school hall. Then, all together, they walk to the church.

The two people have unpacked the greenery. 'It is nearly the season of Advent,' they explain. 'It is the countdown to Christmas – the time when people remember the birth of Jesus Christ. We are going to make an Advent crown to help count the weeks.'

The crown is set in a garden saucer full of soil. Four red candles in flowerpots go around the edge. A tall white candle in a flowerpot is set in the middle. The greenery is arranged in the soil.

The Advent crown is put on a pedestal.

'Here in church, we will light a red candle on each of the next four Sundays to look forward to the coming of Jesus,' one of the grown-ups says. 'We will light the white candle on Christmas Day, to celebrate Jesus' birthday.'

'Can I come and watch?' asks a boy. It is Daniel.

'You can all tell your families that everyone is welcome to come to church any Sunday,' the grown-ups say. 'If you come, you can either sit in the main church, or you can stay at the back where there are books and toys to enjoy if the service seems a bit long.'

That Sunday, Daniel comes to church with his mum and his gran. He is asked to help light the first candle.

9 Getting Ready for Christmas

Through December, all the school helps to make a Christmas crib scene for the carol service in church.

Year 6 paint two enormous boxes to look like a stable.

Year 5 make a stand-up Mary and Joseph.

Year 4 paint two boxes to look like a manger and fill it with hay. They also make an ox and a donkey.

Year 3 make some angels and shepherds.

Year 2 make little animals: doves and mice and spiders.

Year 1 wrap a doll to be the baby Jesus, and learn to sing the carol 'Away in a manger'.

10 The Christmas Carol Service

In the afternoon before the last day of term, everyone goes to the church for a carol service.

The singing group sits in the choir stalls again. They are dressed as angels.

The rest of the school is allowed to dress as angels or shepherds or sheep.

Four of the best readers from Year 6 tell the Christmas story. They stand on something that is rather like a look-out: high enough for them to see everyone, and for everyone to see them. 'It's called the pulpit,' explains Sophie to her classmates.

'It's where the vicar stands to speak to the people.'

Three well-behaved helpers from Year 6 put the crib scene in place as the story is told.

It isn't easy to hear all the words, but here are some…

'Mary and Joseph had to travel to Bethlehem.

'They took shelter in a stable because there was no room at the inn.

'There, Mary had a baby, just as an angel had said. She named the baby Jesus.'

Then comes the bit in the story when an angel tells shepherds that Jesus has been born. All the angels and shepherds and sheep go to the stable to see the baby while the singing group sings carols.

The grown-ups at the back are either smiling a lot or clutching handkerchiefs.

11 Celebrating Christmas

Then it is the holidays.

On Christmas Eve, there is a village procession. It seems that nearly everyone walks from the field beyond the newest houses through the village to the school field.

Some carry burning torches.

Others carry electric torches.

Many of the children are given a lightstick. 'So much safer,' say the mums.

People sing carols and Christmas songs.

They eat roasted chestnuts and mince pies and ginger biscuits.

They drink hot, spicy apple juice.

'And after this,' announces the vicar, 'there will be the Midnight Service of the Nativity in church, by candlelight.'

'Nativity is the posh word for birth,' explains Sophie. 'So a play about the birth of Jesus is a Nativity play, and a crib scene is also called a Nativity scene.'

Not many children are allowed to stay up to go to the church. Sophie and Daniel are some of the lucky ones. They can hardly see among the crowds of people.

In the candlelight, a brass stand called a lectern shines like gold. It is in the shape of an eagle. On the eagle's back is a large book: the Bible. From this book, people read

again the story of the birth of Jesus, and of the night when angels told shepherds that the baby was going to bring joy from heaven to earth.

New Year comes. At midnight, the bellringers in the church ring in the new year.

A few days later, a new term starts.

'In church, the Christmas celebrations are not quite over,' the vicar explains on the first morning. 'This afternoon, you are all invited to the last part.'

The crib scene is still where it was.

'This time in the year is called Epiphany,' says the vicar. 'In church we remember when the wise men came from far-off lands to visit Jesus. The story of their coming reminds people that the Christmas message of joy and peace is for all the world.'

The village shopkeeper, the school caretaker and the new

postman march slowly in. They are dressed in robes made from curtains and tinsel, and look like the wise men on Christmas cards. They are carrying gifts, which they take to the crib.

'Gold, for a king.'

'Frankincense, which burns with a sweet-smelling smoke. It is a gift for a priest, who brings people closer to God.'

'Myrrh, for sprinkling in the grave cloths of an important person. It is a gift for someone whose death is as important as his life.'

The vicar pauses. Then he says, 'Now we are going to give you all a Christingle. It is another reminder of Jesus, and the Christmas message that lights the world.

'The orange stands for the world.

'The sweets stand for the good things the world provides.

'The red ribbon stands for the blood of Jesus: among his own people

were those who did not understand his message and had him put to death.

'The light stands for Jesus and his message, which lights the world.'

Everyone is given a lit Christingle.

One of the boys has kept a Christmas lightstick for this moment, to use instead of a candle.

13 Shrove Tuesday

The winter weeks are cold and grey.

'Nasty weather,' the curate calls out one morning as the children walk to school. The sleet is blowing in their faces. 'We'll have a party this afternoon.'

A team of grown-ups comes to the dinner hall at lunchtime. They take flour and sugar, butter, eggs and milk and begin to mix pancakes.

Soon they have cooked a great pile of them!

Some are for pancake games: toss the pancake, run with the pancake, throw the pancake.

Most are for eating: with lemon and sugar, or sticky syrup.

'Today is Shrove Tuesday,' says the curate. 'The tradition is for people to use up their rich foods by making pancakes, so that from tomorrow they can live more simply through the seven weeks of Lent.'

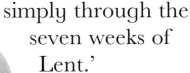

14 Ash Wednesday

The day after Pancake day seems very quiet. But as the children walk home from school, they see people leaving the church with black smudges on their foreheads.

No one knows why.

'Why is your face dirty?' a toddler in a pushchair asks a grey-haired lady.

Everyone gathers round to hear the answer.

'Today is Ash Wednesday,' she explains. 'It is the beginning of Lent. The story is that when Jesus grew up, he spent forty days without food thinking about how to live as God wanted him to. In Lent, some people live simply too, and think extra hard about how to live as God wants.'

'So is that why rich foods get eaten on Pancake day?' asks a boy, and the lady says yes.

'But why is your face dirty?' asks the toddler again.

'A long time ago,' says the lady, 'people used to wear sackcloth and put ashes on their head to show they were sorry for the wrong things they had done. On Ash Wednesday, we keep the old tradition by having a mark of ash made on our heads.'

'What did you do wrong?' asks the toddler. His mum says hush, but the lady laughs.

'I am not always as kind as I could be,' she says.

'Neither am I,' says Daniel.

The others are surprised. 'You're one of the nicest boys in the school,' says a girl.

'True,' say her friends. 'You don't push and shove, and you never cheat.'

'Well, perhaps Lent is a good time for people to decide for themselves if they're doing right things or wrong things,' smiles the lady.

15 The Church Family in Lent

The weeks of Lent go on and on. One afternoon in school, everyone makes a card for their mother.

'And my dad, and my gran, and my aunt who isn't a mum, and the lady next door.' Sophie is good at cards, and she makes one for everyone 'who is real family or as good as family'.

There is a big notice inviting everyone to come to church that Sunday.

A lot of families come. For Sophie's friend Lisa, it is her first time in church on a Sunday.

A choir dressed in white robes sits in the choir stalls. The curate and the vicar are wearing long robes too.

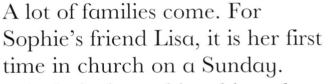

They read from the Bible on the lectern.

There is a talk from the pulpit.

There is kneeling for prayers.

There is standing to sing hymns.

'Today is Mothering Sunday,' announces the curate. 'It is also the day that Peter and Sarah Heffer – Jamie's mum and dad – have brought their new baby Laura to be baptized. I want the family and the godparents to come to the font, and all the children to gather round.'

So a crowd stands in a circle around a huge stone basin.

The parents and godparents

of the baby make promises.

The vicar makes the sign of a cross in water on the baby's forehead, saying that he baptizes her in the name of the Father, the Son and the Holy Spirit.

'Called God for short,' adds Daniel to Lisa.

Then it is back to Mothering Sunday. Someone has been busy making posies and there is a lot of rushing about to hand out posies to mums and (as Sophie said) everyone who is family or as good as family.

'Actually,' says Lisa to Sophie's mum later, 'we ended up giving posies to everyone.'

'Well, a church really is a family,' says the curate.

16 Palm Sunday

Towards the end of March comes exciting news.

On Sunday, the churchpeople will act out a Bible story about Jesus. The curate explains that the Christmas baby, Jesus, grew to be a man. Then, one day, he went away…

'I know! He spent forty days thinking about what to do with the rest of his life,' adds Daniel.

'True,' she agrees. 'There came a time when he stopped working at the trade he learned from Joseph…'

'Who was a carpenter,' says Lisa.

'Indeed; and he decided to do the job he was born for: to help people love God more.

'He began to teach and preach. Crowds followed him to listen to his stories and his teaching. Others came to see him work miracles: he healed many people with a touch; he took food for one and it became enough to feed thousands.

'He had many friends, and a lot of people thought he was going to be a great hero for his people and set them free from the Romans. The story we are telling on Sunday is about the time Jesus came to the city of Jerusalem riding on a donkey, with crowds of

people watching and cheering.'

A donkey is part of the story. She spends the week practising.

On Sunday, the whole village comes to see.

The donkey does her part very well.

The person who plays Jesus is smiling but looks scared.

The choir try to sing and walk. It doesn't work.

The crowds cheer.

'A horse would have been more exciting,' says a boy.

'That's the point,' says the vicar. 'A hero coming to lead a rebellion would have come on a horse. Jesus rode a little donkey. It was a sign he was coming in peace.'

Some of the crowd wave palm leaves. They have been sent from a hot country far away and are dry and pale. 'When the story really happened, people cut fresh leaves,' explains the curate.

'When the story really happened, people threw down their real cloaks,' explains the vicar.

Some women are waiting with old curtains for the bit when the donkey goes right into the church. They throw the curtains down, but in this case it is to protect the carpet.

Then the donkey goes right into the church and up to the front, carrying 'Jesus'. In the church service there are prayers, hymns and readings, but a lot of people are really looking at the donkey.

17 Good Friday

'What happened to Jesus when he got to Jerusalem?' the children want to know the next day at school. The vicar has come to give the talk in the hall.

'He went on as usual, teaching people and working miracles that brought good things. But he also got into trouble. The things he did upset many of the religious leaders of his people. They were not sure his teaching was right. They didn't want to believe that his miracles were from God.

'So they wanted to get rid of him. They told lies to make the Roman governor think Jesus was a rebel and was going to make trouble for him.'

'Even though he rode a donkey?'

'That's right. It was a lie, but it worked. In the end, the governor, Pontius Pilate, agreed to have him put to death. The punishment was crucifixion: Jesus was nailed to a cross of wood.'

'Is that why there are crosses everywhere in church?' asks a boy.

'It is,' says the vicar.

Year 3 visit the church later that day. Their project is to draw all the crosses they can find.

The next day all the drawings are on display in the hall.

'This Friday,' says the vicar, 'is the day we will have a very quiet service in church to remember the day Jesus died. It's called Good Friday.'

'There's nothing good about a good person dying,' says a girl.

The vicar agrees. 'But on Sunday comes Easter, and there's going to be good news.'

Only Daniel goes to the church on Friday. The service is quiet, with solemn singing. Daniel remembers his gran's friend. My friend too, he thinks. I like the music, because I feel I'm not alone in my sadness.

Easter Sunday feels like the first morning of spring. The sun shines and a thousand daffodils have opened.

The bell-ringers ring the church bells for half an hour before church.

Daniel is the first child to arrive in church. For the first time in weeks, it is filled with flowers.

The readings from the Bible tell the story of Easter.

After Jesus died, his friends took the body and put it in a stone tomb. After the day of rest, the sabbath, some of his friends went to say goodbye for the last time. They found the tomb open and the body gone. They saw Jesus alive! Sophie's mum, the curate, gives the talk. She says that Jesus' coming alive shows that there is a way to heaven for everyone.

At the back of the church, Daniel, Sophie and Lisa each try to draw a picture of what heaven is like. They finish just in time for a ceremony called Holy Communion.

'I've never seen this happen before,' whispers Lisa.

'Oh, the night before Jesus died, Jesus shared a meal with his

friends and told them always to share bread and wine and remember him. That's what we do,' says Sophie.

'You know so much,' sighs Daniel.

Sophie shrugs. 'What you know about church isn't really important,' she says. 'Mum says it's only following Jesus that matters.'

The children are invited to go to the front during communion: through the screen with the cross above it, past the choir, to the rail. Beyond is a table covered with white cloth, called an altar.

The vicar and curate and some other helpers offer people a sip of wine and some bread.

The children decide to stand to one side, and the vicar says a prayer to each of them, asking for God's blessing.

Soon it is time for a loud hymn… and then Easter eggs are given to all the children!

19 The Pentecost Picnic

When the summer term begins, the vicar comes to the school and tells the Easter story again.

Daniel already has a question.

'What happened to Jesus afterwards?'

The vicar explains: for forty days, Jesus came to talk with his friends. He told them to go on telling people the message he had given: to love God and one another.

Then, one day, Jesus was lifted up to heaven. The church has a

service to remember that day: Ascension Day.

On a special Thursday, everyone goes from school to the church to listen to the story the curate tells them.

Jesus was with his friends. Then a cloud wrapped itself round him and he was taken to heaven.

The curate adds, 'In a way, heaven begins here and now when people live as God's friends.'

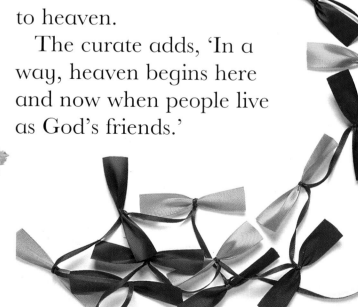

She talks more about that on the Friday of the next week.

'After Jesus went to heaven, his friends felt rather alone and scared. Ten days later came a festival called Pentecost. On that day, Jesus' closest friends heard the sound of rushing wind and saw flames above their heads. They believed this was the sign of God's Holy Spirit coming to them. Suddenly they felt brave enough to start telling people about Jesus… it felt rather as if God was their secret invisible friend. The followers of Jesus have said the same thing ever since.'

She says that the church is celebrating Pentecost on Sunday with a service and then a picnic in the vicarage garden. It is a warm and sunny day in June.

'It's a bit windy for a picnic,' says one of the mums.

'A bit,' agrees the curate, 'but a great day for kites.'

They make red and yellow paper kites with streamers.

'A reminder of the flames of Pentecost,' says Daniel.

20 The Wedding of the Year

In the middle of July comes a very special day. The Year 2 teacher, Miss Bridges, is getting married in the church – and starting her holiday early!

The week before, her mother and her sisters are at the church every day, making it look lovely.

On the day, the guests arrive in very smart clothes. They sit in the pews at the front.

Everyone in school comes to church and sits in the places that are left.

The bridegroom is already at the church with his best man.

Then, at noon, the bride arrives.

Everyone is quiet. The organist plays a march and the bride comes with her father and some bridesmaids. They walk up the aisle.

The vicar leads the ceremony. The bride and groom make

promises and give each other a gold ring.

Then they go out past the choir stalls to sign the register. While they are out, Year 2 go to the front with the music teacher, Mrs Rowlands. The teacher plays the piano and the children sing a song. When the bride and groom are ready to come back through the church, they sing another song specially for the bride.

'Thank you,' she says. 'I asked Mrs Rowlands to play the piano, but I didn't realize you were all going to sing. It was lovely.' The children are pleased and smile at one another. Then they rush to their seats, and the bride and groom and all the family march out through the church.

Afterwards, everyone has tea and cakes in the school hall. Then the wedding party goes off to a smart hotel for dinner and a dance.

21 The School Year Ends

The end of term comes. On the last but one afternoon, everyone goes to the church again. The grown-ups sit at the back.

'We have come to say goodbye to Year 6, and to celebrate another year in our lives,' explains the headteacher.

Each year group brings a display of some of the things they have done. Everyone in the school can see one of their best ever pieces of work on show. Then the head says this:

'This school was founded over a hundred years ago by churchgoers who wanted Clove to have its own school. They wanted all the children in the village to have a good start, because they believed, as I believe, that every person is special to God. Over the year, we learn from things the church does, and the church learns from things that we do. And now, I am going to read a new prayer. It was written by Daniel, as he sat in church one Sunday. I think it is rather nice...'

Dear God

You understand good times and bad times.
You bring harvest and Christmas and Easter and lots more.
You give us lots to learn and lots to think about.
You are older than anything:
older than the big oak tree,
older than the yew tree.
Help us to grow good as we grow older.

Amen.